Chambers

Letter Writing

Isobel E. Williams

Chambers

Other titles in this series

Chambers Effective English
Chambers English Grammar
Chambers Good English
Chambers Good Spelling
Chambers Idioms
Chambers Phrasal Verbs

Published 1991 by W & R Chambers Ltd,
43–45 Annandale Street, Edinburgh EH7 4AZ

Reprinted 1992, 1993

British Library Cataloguing in Publication Data

A catalogue record for this book is
available from the British Library

ISBN 0-550-18037-0

Typeset by Alphaset Graphics Ltd, Edinburgh
Printed and bound in Great Britain by
Cox & Wyman Ltd, Reading, Berkshire

Contents

Introduction

The written word is one of the surest and commonest ways of passing on information. It ranges from the quickly scribbled note, through memoranda, letters, pamphlets and brochures, to newspapers, magazines and books.

Although letter writing is being superseded by telecommunications and although more messages, particularly personal messages, are communicated by telephone, the letter still survives. Writing a letter offers several advantages. Among them are that:

- ideas can be fully explained;
- there is a record for reference and for legal purposes;
- identical copies can be distributed to several people at one time.

At some time in their life everyone has to write letters: a job application, a letter of complaint or a letter of condolence to a friend. However, whatever the type of letter, almost everyone has had the experience of staring at a blank piece of paper and wondering how to begin.

This book shows you how to write letters of all sorts, making suggestions about how to get your message across simply and effectively. It advises on layout and writing materials, and it includes tips about spelling, punctuation and grammar.

The general principles of letter writing are outlined and demonstrated before specific types of letters are dealt with. Each letter section gives rules for the type of letter covered before giving some example letters. Each section also contains a set of useful phrases which can be adapted to suit the needs of your own particular letters.

This book is not just for secretaries or businessmen, but for everyone who must at some time write a letter. It is also a useful guide for non-native speakers of English and can be used as a complementary handbook by EFL students who are studying for Cambridge First Certificate or Chamber of Commerce examinations.

The rules and methods outlined in this book will help you to write letters on any subject and to know that your letters will be understood.

Common mistakes are indicated with an asterisk *.

1
Making a Start

Although a phone call is quick and easy, saves energy and frustration and almost always ensures an instant response, there are times when *only* written communication will do. In business, important messages may be forgotten and instructions which are long and complicated risk being misunderstood if they are not written down; a written record is usually needed for orders and offers; a message which has to be distributed among a number of people working in different offices can only be transmitted in writing. Personal letters to friends you have not seen for a long time or to an elderly relative are often more appreciated than a quick phone call and, for those with friends abroad a letter is the most economical way of keeping in touch.

Whoever you are writing to, your letter should be:

- well typed or clearly handwritten;
- written on good quality paper;
- properly set out;
- well structured;
- polite and courteous.

Before you start to write:

- think clearly about your objectives and what you want to say (it may be, at this point, that you decide that a phone call will serve your purpose better);

- if you decide that your message *must* be written down, note all the points you want to get across and use these notes to make a rough draft. Failure to do this will result in a muddled letter which will only cause confusion and frustration.

When writing the letter:

- write clearly and logically;
- remember that each separate idea belongs in a paragraph by itself;
- always check spelling and grammar if you are unsure.

In business:

- be brief, but include all the necessary information and think about the recipient: Will they understand what you mean? Do they have all the background information?
- give your letter or memo a heading – this helps the recipient to see at once what you are writing about;
- if the information is complicated, number the paragraphs – this helps the reader understand and makes a reply easier.

2

Writing Materials

It is not only the content, but also the *visual impression* created when your letter is read for the first time that determines how much attention the recipient will give to your message. If a letter does not look good when it comes out of the envelope, it can put the reader off straight away.

In a busy office an illegible scrawl will, at best, be put aside to be dealt with later, and at worst be relegated to the wastepaper-basket immediately. Mismatched paper and envelope, typing mistakes and bad handwriting all give as bad an impression as spelling mistakes and poor English.

The same is true for a personal letter. First impressions count.

Handwritten or Typed?

Most personal letters are handwritten, though someone who has bad eyesight will appreciate a clearly typed personal letter.

Unless your handwriting is *very* clear, use a typewriter when writing to people who have English as a second or foreign language. Problems with the English language are made worse by illegible handwriting, which will cause frustration and misunderstanding.

When typing a personal letter use roman or normal type. A 'cursive' or italic type can never truly imitate handwriting and is often difficult to read.

The following letters should always be handwritten:

- letters of condolence;
- job applications which are asked for in the applicant's own hand.

When writing by hand:

- write in a legible flowing script but do not add flourishes or decorations;
- use a fountain pen or Biro with blue or black ink. Never use a pencil or felt-tip pen.

Notepaper and Envelopes

Notepaper should be of good quality, unlined, unbleached or in white or cream. The envelope should match the paper.

Private correspondence is usually written on plain, unheaded notepaper though some people have their address and telephone number printed at the top of their notepaper. Printing can be expensive, however, so if you write very few letters or only to close friends it is extravagant to invest in printed notepaper. Businesses always use headed notepaper, with the firm's name, address and other details clearly printed.

Paper sizes have been standardized. Most firms use A4 paper (210×297 mm) which should fit inside an envelope with a maximum of two folds.

Sizes
A0 = 841 × 1189 mm
A1 = 594 × 841 mm
A2 = 420 × 594 mm
A3 = 297 × 420 mm
A4 = 210 × 297 mm
A5 = 148 × 210 mm
A6 = 105 × 148 mm
A7 = 74 × 105 mm

Types of paper

Bond – a good quality paper which should not crease or tear easily. Usually white although pastel colours are obtainable. Used for top copy and business correspondence, when the firm's letterheading is printed at the top of the page. Normal weight 70–90 gsm (grammes per square metre).

A0

A1

A2

A3

A4

A5

A6

A7

A7

Airmail – a thin lightweight paper which reduces the cost of overseas airmail postage.

Bank – a flimsy paper used for carbon copies and sets of forms. White or coloured and weighing 40–50 gsm. When regular multi-person/-department distributions are made, coloured copies can be made to identify specific areas.

NCR (no carbon required) – the reverse side of the top copy and top sides of subsequent sheets are treated with a special substance to produce copies.

With the widespread use of photocopying machines, Bank and NCR papers are being used less and less.

Types of envelopes

Post Office Preferred (POP) envelopes and cards – there is a preferred range of sizes known as POP which is based on suitability for Royal Mail equipment. This range is recommended for all users, business and private. To fall within the POP range envelopes must be:

- no smaller than 90 × 140 mm;
- no bigger than 120 × 235 mm;
- oblong in shape; the longer side should be at least 1.4 times the shorter side;
- made from paper weighing at least 63 gsm including contents.

The most widely used International Standards Organization envelope sizes, ie DL (110 × 220 mm) and C6 (114 × 162 mm), fall within the POP range.

The above rules apply equally to window envelopes and cards, which should be rigid.

Other types of envelope – a stock of the following shapes in varying sizes should be kept in the stationery store of every business enterprise.

Window and aperture envelopes save time as the name

and address do not have to be typed twice, but care must be taken to position the address correctly so that no detail is lost. Enclosures must then be secured in such a way that they do not move and obscure the address.

Other types of envelope

Banker		opens on the longer side
Pocket		opens on the shorter side
Window		a cut out address panel covered with transparent material
Aperture		a cut out address panel NOT covered with transparent material

Addressing an Envelope

As much care should be taken with addressing an envelope as with writing a letter.

The address should be written neatly and clearly with the envelope horizontal. In modern business, addresses are usually written in block form with all the information lined up on the left-hand side. Commas are not used.

Start the address halfway down the envelope to leave plenty of room for stamps and franking. *Personal* or *Confidential* is written to the left above the name of the addressee, if needed. If you are writing to a person in a large organization always add the department or office name.

The Post Office specifies a correct posting address for every delivery point and advises the following address format:

1. *Name of the addressee.*
2. *Number of house* (or name of the house if it does not have

a number) and street name. These two pieces of information must always be included in the address. If the recipient of the letter lives in a flat or if the letter is being sent to a suite of offices, the number of the flat or suite, the floor on which it is located, and the number or name of the block of which the premises form part should also be included in the address.

3. *Locality name* (where applicable). The name of a locality is sometimes needed in addition to the post town to distinguish between streets of the same name in the same postal delivery area.

4. *Post town* in block capitals. A post town acts as a clearing point for a particular district and is the basic unit of the postal delivery system. It must therefore always be included in the address and shown in block capitals.

5. *County name or region* (where applicable).

6. *Postcode*. Every address in the UK and many other countries has a postcode. The postcode is a summary of an address, which, converted into machine-readable language, enables mail to be electronically sorted. The postcode consists of groups of letters and numbers, and forms the last item of an address. Remember:

- always show the postcode as the last item of an address, if possible on a line by itself;
- always type or write a postcode in block capitals;
- do not use any punctuation marks in the postcode;
- leave a space, equivalent to at least one character, between the two parts of the postcode;
- never underline the postcode;
- do not join the characters of the postcode in any way;
- if it is impossible to place the postcode on a separate line, it should be written on the same line as the county name or post town. It should, however, be separated from whatever precedes it by a space equivalent to at least two and preferably six characters.

7. *The name of the country of destination* should be written in the language of the country of posting.

In most EC countries and in America it is common to write the address of the sender on the back of the envelope if the envelope does not carry the logo and address of the firm.

Special mailing instructions (AE = American English term, BE = British English term, EC = European Community term):

- *airmail* – to be transported by plane;
- *certified mail* (AE) – similar to *registered mail*, but uninsured;
- *express* – parcels, freight, letters, money etc travel faster by this method than by ordinary mail service;
- *general delivery* (AE), *poste restante* (EC) – postal service delivering mail to a specific post office where it is held for collection by an addressee;
- POB – Post Office Box;
- *POP* – Post Office Preferred;
- *postcode, zip code* (AE) – letters and figures written directly after the address;
- *printed matter* – newspapers, books, brochures, etc which may be sent at reduced rates;
- *registered post, registered mail* (AE) – provides evidence of posting and gives added protection for valuable and important mail;
- special delivery – delivery of an item of mail by a special carrier before it would ordinarily arrive in the next normal postal delivery.

3

Making Yourself Understood

Drafts

A letter which is written in bad English will be difficult to understand, particularly if sentences are not properly punctuated, words are inappropriate or badly spelled and grammar is misleading.

A letter can also be confusing because of unclear thinking on the part of the writer. In many letters:

- there is no introduction to give the reader an immediate indication of content;
- the ideas are not in any particular order;
- the relation between ideas is not clear;
- there is no conclusion.

You can make sure that your letters are clear and understandable by first writing a draft.

Take a piece of scrap paper and note down the following:

- the objectives of the letter;
- the main points to be made;
- any firm conclusions to be conveyed.

When you have noted down all the points to be covered, number them in order of importance. If you have included any irrelevant information, score it out. Refer to these notes frequently when writing your draft.

When you have finished your draft:

- check that all the points have been covered in a logical order;

- check that all the information is complete and correct;
- check the spelling or meaning of any words you are unsure of.

Only when you have done all that should you write the letter.

Have the following books beside you when you write:

- an English dictionary or good spelling guide;
- an English usage dictionary;

and refer to them when necessary.

When you have finished your letter reread it several times, asking yourself the following questions:

- Will the recipient understand the letter?
- Have all the important facts been included?
- Have the main points been expressed?
- Is the letter polite?

If necessary, ask for a second opinion from someone who can offer helpful advice.

Style

Unless you are writing a love letter or a funny letter to a close friend, you should always express your meaning simply and directly, omitting words that are not strictly necessary and making sure that the major points are not lost in minor details.

Use clear and specific vocabulary, avoiding jargon, ambiguous phrases and unnecessarily technical or formal language. Try to avoid needless repetition of either subject or vocabulary; if a word recurs frequently, consult a thesaurus for an alternative.

Form sentences of different lengths and of varied structure, sticking to simple and compound sentences but avoiding overlong sentences. (One way to test for the latter is to read your letter aloud.) Make positive rather than negative statements and use active rather than passive verbs when possible.

Use a separate paragraph to deal with every major subject or idea; within each paragraph, make sure that every sentence connects logically with the preceding one.

Vocabulary

Some people believe that formal words and phrases are impressive and show a good command of English. A letter which is too formal, however, is often difficult to understand. If you use everyday words your message will come across clearly and simply, with no possibility of misunderstanding.

Here is a list of some formal words and phrases and their everyday equivalents.

Formal	*Everyday*
to assist	to help
to cease	to stop
to commence	to begin/to start
to complete	to finish
to deem	to think
to desire	to wish/to want
to endeavour	to try
feasible	possible
to function	to work
to implement	to carry out
to obtain	to get
to peruse	to look at/to read
to proceed	to go
to purchase	to buy
replete (adj)	full
to request	to ask for
to require	to need
to reside	to live
to seek	to try/to look for
sufficient	enough
to transmit	to send
vessel	ship
viable	workable

Sentences

Always remember to:

- start a sentence with a capital letter;
- end a sentence with a full stop, an exclamation mark or a question mark;
- include a subject and verb.

Try as far as possible to:

- stay in one tense;
- place descriptive phrases, adjectives and adverbs as close as possible to their subject.

If you use a pronoun, check that it is clear which subject the pronoun refers to.

There are three types of sentences: simple, compound and complex. A simple sentence expresses only one idea. It has one subject and one object:

The man (subject) sat in his armchair (object).

A compound sentence contains more than one idea, but all the ideas expressed have an equal value:

The man sat in his armchair reading the newspaper.

A complex sentence contains one main idea (the main clause) and one or more secondary ideas (subordinate clauses):

As soon as he came home from work (subordinate clause) the man sat in his armchair and read his newspaper (main clause).

Every finite verb in a sentence marks a separate clause; each clause should be linked to the next by a conjunction, a comma, a colon or a semicolon. Avoid joining a number of clauses with *and* or *but*.

Word order

Because the English language is not inflected, ie it has very few endings on nouns, verbs, etc, it is important to stick to the sentence pattern of Subject (S), Verb (V), Object (O):

John (S) drinks (V) tea (O).

However, a subject may be separated from its verb by an adverb of frequency, eg *generally, sometimes, often, frequently, rarely, seldom, always, usually, (n)ever, occasionally, already, just, still*:

John *usually* drinks tea.

Inversion

If a word or phrase like *never, not only, nowhere, not until, little, less, only, rarely, seldom . . . when, hardly . . . when, no sooner . . . than* is placed at the beginning of a sentence the sentence pattern must be inverted:

No sooner had I arrived than the telephone began to ring.

Inversion is often used to make things sound dramatic and may have a place in a private letter. However, it is best avoided in business letters:

The telephone began to ring as soon as I arrived.

Paragraphs

A good rule is: one idea, one paragraph. If you have difficulty in deciding when to start a new paragraph, ask yourself at the start of every sentence: Is the next sentence on the same theme as the one I have just written? If the answer is 'No', then you can start a new paragraph.

In the following example letter there are three distinct topics:

1. The subject of the letter.
2. Information about delivery.
3. Terms of payment.

The letter ends with a formal closing statement (4.).

Dear Sir/Madam

1. Thank you for your letter of 23 April 1990 asking for our current catalogue and price list, which you will find enclosed.

2. Goods which are delivered from stock are usually sent within a week of receipt of order. Delivery time for special orders is slightly longer.

3. Our usual terms of payment are ninety days from the date of delivery.

4. We are sure that our pure wool pullovers will find a ready market with your customers because of their good quality, excellent workmanship and traditional design and we look forward to receiving your first order.

Yours faithfully

Correct Grammatical Usage
Who/whom

1. Use the pronoun *who* when it refers to the subject of the sentence:

    The *man* (subject) *who* phoned yesterday came to the office today.

2. Use the pronoun *whom* when it refers to the object of the sentence:

    The *man* (object) *whom* you (subject) phoned yesterday came to the office today.

3. Use *whom* when the pronoun is governed by a preposition – try to keep the preposition and the pronoun together:

    The man *to whom* you spoke on the phone yesterday came to the office today.

Like/as

1. Use *like* to compare things or people, ie to qualify nouns or pronouns:

   Your *pen* is like *mine*.

   My *sewing machine* is like *Anne's*.

   She looks like a *woman* I met in Spain. (Here two people are compared.)

2. Use *as* to compare actions, ie to join clauses and thus govern verbs. Sometimes the verb is only implied.

   Jenny thinks very much as I *do*.

   Press the off button as I *told* you.

   We shall give Granny handkerchiefs, as *we did* last year.

Due to, owing to, because of

1. Use *due to* only when preceded by some tense of the verb 'to be':

   My illness *was* due to a virus.

   If the firm succeeds it *will be* due to their hard work.

2. Do not begin a sentence with *due to*. It is better to use 'because of'.

3. If a choice can be made between the phrases *because of*, *owing to* and *due to*, use the first. *Owing to* and *due to* often cause ugly as well as dubious constructions.

Shall/should, will/would

1. When making a statement of fact without special emphasis, *I* and *we* are usually followed by *shall* or *should*; *you, he, she, it* and *they* are followed by *will* or *would*:

   I *shall* be happy to meet you at the station.

   We *should* be grateful if you *would* write to us without delay.

   Will she get the job or *will* they give it to someone else?

2. *Shall* is used with *will* (future tense):

   I *shall* be glad if you *will* let me have a reply at once.

   If you *will* let us have your cheque we *shall* send the goods immediately.

I/me

1. Use *I* as the subject of a sentence:

   I like to sing in the bath.

   Mistakes often occur when *I* or *me* is linked with another noun or pronoun. Avoid these mistakes by mentally taking away the intervening noun or pronoun and checking that what remains makes sense:

   Please meet (the managing director and) *me* for an interview.

   Not: * Please meet (the managing director and) *I* for an interview.

2. Use *I* if the pronoun is linked to a following clause:

   It was *I* who wrote the report.

3. Use *me* after a preposition:

   Come *with me*.

   Give it *to me*.

   Mistakes sometimes happen when the object of a preposition is two pronouns linked by 'and':

   Between you and *me*. (*Not*:* Between you and *I*.)

   Like you and *me*. (*Not*:* Like you and *I*.)

Either/or, neither/nor

1. Use *either* or *neither* with two persons or things:

   I have examined both machines and find that *either* (*neither*) will suit our purpose.

2. Use *either* or *neither* with the singular. Both words refer to one person or thing to the exclusion of the other:

   You will find that *either* (*neither*) of the applicants *is* suitable.

3. Always follow *either* by *or*, and *neither* by *nor*, in a comparison:

   Either (*neither*) Richard *or* (*nor*) David is to be given the prize.

4. Always place *either* or *neither* next to the words they qualify:

   I shall buy *either* (*neither*) a magazine *or* (*nor*) a newspaper.

   Not: * I shall *either* (*neither*) buy a magazine *or* (*nor*) a newspaper.

Each/none

Use *each* and *none* with the singular as they refer to one person or thing:

Each of you *is* to receive a rise in salary next month.

As *none* of the clerks *is* willing to work overtime we are behind schedule this week.

Much/many, less/few

1. *Much* and *less* are used with uncountables and abstracts:

   How *much time* do you have?

   There is *less traffic* on the roads nowadays.

2. *Many* and *few* are used with countables:

   I have so *many things* to do today.

   Very *few people* came to the party.

The infinitive

The infinitive has two forms: present and past:

to do (present infinitive)

to have done (past infinitive)

1. Use the present infinitive after a past tense or any compound tense:

   I meant *to telephone* you yesterday.

   Not: * I meant to have telephoned you yesterday.

   The staff would have preferred *to work* a five-day week.

   Not: * The staff would have preferred to have worked a five-day week.

2. Use the past infinitive when the present tense is followed by an infinitive which describes a past event:

   Henry Ford *is said to have been* a millionaire by the age of forty.

The split infinitive

The infinitive of a verb consists of two words, eg *to forecast*, *to announce*, *to move*. The two words are *one unit* and should not be separated (split) by the insertion of additional words or phrases. Opinions differ on the gravity of this error but all agree that gross infringements of the rule should be avoided:

I should like, on behalf of our members, *to move* a vote of thanks to the chairman.

Not: * I should like *to*, on behalf of our members, *move* a vote of thanks to the chairman.

Comparative and superlative

The comparative or the superlative is formed:
by adding *-er* or *-est* to one-syllable words:
small, small*er*, small*est*;
by using *more* or *most* with words of more than one syllable:
more beautiful, *most* beautiful;
or by using the correct irregular form:
good, better, best;
bad, worse, worst.

1. Use the comparative degree when two things are compared, and the superlative for more than two:
    Mary has taken the *better* of the two typewriters and the *best* of the three chairs.
    Which of these two cloths is the *more* hard-wearing?
2. Use *less* for quantity or amount; use *fewer* for number:
    The car industry has bought *less steel* than it did last year and thus produced *fewer cars*.
    I paid £100 *less* than the market price for my new computer.
3. *Unique* means the only one of its kind and has no comparative. It should not be used casually to mean novel, scarce or rare. 'Almost unique' is allowable, but * 'comparatively unique' or * 'very unique' reduce the word to absurdity and should not be used.

Verbal nouns (gerunds)

Verbal nouns are nouns which are made by adding *-ing* to the verb.

The chairman likes *travelling*.
They hate *leaving* work unfinished.
Taking a holiday is very refreshing.

1. Qualify verbal nouns by possessive adjectives, not by pronouns, ie *my, his, our, your, their*, not * me, * him, * us, * you, * them.

    The error was caused by *his typing* so carelessly.

    The accident was caused by *your driving* too fast.

    Do you agree to *my taking* a day off tomorrow?

2. Use the possessive form for a noun qualifying a verbal noun:

    I don't object to *Mary's talking* provided she lowers her voice.

    He is unemployed because of the *firm's going* into liquidation.

    The department has been disorganized by the *manager's leaving*.

Conjunctions

Words which are used to combine sentences are called conjunctions. The main conjunctions which are used to form compound sentences are: *and, but, yet, so, both . . . and, (n)either . . . (n)or, not only . . . but.*

1. The word *and* is used to relate two statements which have the same meaning, whereas *but* is used to indicate a contrast or a difference:

    Mary *and* John *will both* come to the party.

    Mary *will come* to the party *but* John won't.

2. Neither *and* nor *but* should come at the beginning of a sentence in a business letter. Instead of using *but* at the beginning of a sentence, use *however* followed by a comma:

    The travel agency has lowered its prices and is offering a lot of new package tours. *However*, no one seems to be making any bookings.

Punctuation
Full stop, question mark, exclamation mark

A *full stop* (.) is used at the end of a statement and often after a command; a *question mark* (?) comes after a question and an *exclamation mark* (!) after an exclamation or interjection, and sometimes after a command:

This is a useful report. Show it to the chairman tomorrow.
Would you make a copy for me?
Bye! Don't forget to clean your shoes before you go out!

Comma

A *comma* (,) shows a slight break in a sentence. It is used in the following ways:

1. Between two clauses joined by *but* or *or* if the second clause has a subject:

    I'll come to see you tomorrow, but I (subject) don't know when I'll arrive.

2. After a subordinate clause:

    When he returned, I made a cup of tea.

3. Round the kind of relative clause that gives additional information:

    The salesman, *who had driven from Southampton*, was tired.

    but *not* around the kind of relative clause that identifies a person or thing:

    The people *who would like tickets* should write to the secretary.

    Check whether commas are necessary by mentally removing the relative clause. If the sentence makes sense without the relative clause commas are needed.

4. Around a descriptive or explanatory phrase referring to a person or thing:

    Mrs Cook, *our local councillor*, has joined the committee.

5. After introductory words, or around words which form a comment:

    However, I wasn't late after all.

    I must leave now, *unfortunately*.

    Philip, *I'm sorry to say*, has left the company.

6. Before *please*, after *yes* and *no*, and before or after the name of the person being spoken to:

    May I see the file, *please*?

    No, I'm sorry.

    Hurry up, *James*.

7. In a list of more than two things and often between adjectives preceding a noun, where there are two or more:

a pen, a pencil and a rubber;
a busy, overcrowded room.

Colon

A *colon* (:) is used to introduce the answer that the first part of the sentence expects:

There's one thing I'd really like: a new car.
You'll need the following: a passport, ticket, boarding pass.

Semicolon

A *semicolon* (;) separates parts of a sentence that are equally important and are not linked by *and*, *but*, *or*, etc. Sometimes a semicolon is used to separate items in a list:

One tray of sandwiches will do; to prepare more would be wasteful.
I have three ambitions: to set up my own business; to buy a boat and sail round the world; to live in Sydney.

Quotation marks

Quotation marks (" ") or (' '), also called *inverted commas*, are used before and after direct speech; both sets are written at the same level, slightly above the words which they refer to:

Mary said, 'You're late.'
'You're late,' said Mary, 'and you're in trouble. The boss has been looking for you for ages.'

Both single and double quotation marks are correct, but modern usage prefers single quotation marks. However, if there is a quotation or highlighted passage within another quotation, both single and double quotation marks must be used:

'Did she say, "You're late"?' John asked.

Apostrophe

An *apostrophe* (') is used:

1. To form possessive nouns; it is added, together with an *s*, to singular nouns and to irregular plural nouns (ie those not ending in -*s*):

    Anne'*s* desk, the women'*s* coats.

    If a singular noun ends in -*s* the written form of the possessive echoes the spoken form. Thus we have:

    James'*s* watch but Moses' brother.

    With regular plural nouns (ie those formed by adding *s*) and with expressions of time in which the time expression is treated as a possessive, place the apostrophe after the *s*:

    the residents' car park; the boys' kite;
    three weeks' time.

    Using the possessive apostrophe will cause no problems as long as you remember the following:
    - if there is no *s* at the end of the word, add apostrophe *s*;
    - if the word ends in -*s*, add apostrophe *s* unless no *s* is added in pronunciation in which case add only the apostrophe.
2. In shortened forms, showing where part of a word has been left out:

    I'*ve* (I have) only two appointments today.

    It is*n't* (is not) possible.

    It is very unusual to use shortened forms in business letters.

Hyphen

A *hyphen* (-) is used:

1. After prefixes, especially where the addition of the prefix results in a double vowel:

    anti-freeze, *ex*-president, *pro*-monetarism, *self*-employed, *co-o*perative, *pre-*emptive, *re-*educate.
2. In compound adjectives placed before a noun:

    a *six-page* contract, a *twenty-year-old* building, a *well-deserved* award.
3. To connect a group of words made up of an attributive noun and a noun:

air-conditioning, *motor*-cyclist, *blood*-pressure.

However, when the elements are monosyllabic, the hyphen is omitted and the group written either as one compound word or two separate words:

aircraft, air force, bloodstream, blood cell.

Reading aloud may help to decide if two monosyllabic elements should be written together or separately. If the words run together smoothly, write them as one word. If there is a clash between the last letter of the first word and the first letter of the second word, write them as two words:

They are going to drill some more *oil wells* on the Alaska *oilfield*.

Where British spelling uses a hyphen, American spelling very often writes one word.

4. A hyphen is also used to split a word at the end of a line. Follow these rules:
   - do not split words of only one syllable, eg * ma-rk, * dra-ins;
   - split words at natural breaks, eg some-times, type-writer;
   - do not split names, eg * Ali-stair, * Rich-ard;
   - the first letter on the next line should be a consonant if possible.

There are no spaces before or after a hyphen.

Figures/Currency Signs

Unless writing a bill or a list of comparisons, in which case figures should be used, numbers may be in words up to 100 and thereafter in figures.

Figures may be written without commas: four-figure numbers closed up, as in *4500*; five-figure and above with a thin space, as in *35 000*.

Though we *say* 'ten pounds', 'five dollars', etc, the currency sign comes before the figure when writing:
eg £*10*; *$5*.

Spelling Rules

To a great extent the ability to spell English words correctly depends on becoming familiar with the *look* of them when they are spelled in the accepted way. There are a few general rules, *though always be on the lookout for exceptions*. If in doubt *always* look up words in a dictionary. It is worth while investing in Chambers *Pocket Guide to Good Spelling*.

Words ending in -y

1. The plural of a noun ending in *-y*, *-ay*, *-ey*, *-oy*, *-uy*:

   A noun ending in *-y* following a consonant has the plural *-ies*:

   bab*y*, bab*ies*; countr*y*, countr*ies*

   Nouns ending in *-ay*, *-ey*, *oy*, *uy*, have their plural in *-ays*, *-eys*, etc.

   d*ay*, d*ays*; Mond*ay*, Mond*ays*; donk*ey*, donk*eys*; vall*ey*, vall*eys*; all*oy*, all*oys*; g*uy*, g*uys*

2. The parts of a verb when the verb ends in *-y*, *-ay*, *-ey*, etc:

   The formation is similar to that of noun plurals in 1. above.

   cr*y*, cr*ies*, cr*ied*; certif*y*, certif*ies*, certif*ied*

   but del*ay*, del*ays*, del*ayed*; conv*ey*, conv*eys*, conv*eyed*; destr*oy*, destr*oys*, destr*oyed*; b*uy*, b*uys*

3. Comparison of adjectives, or the formation of nouns or adverbs from them:

   A rule similar to the one above holds for words in *-y*, and in some cases for those in *-ey*, *-oy*, etc:

   shad*y*, shad*ier*, shad*iest*, shad*iness*, shad*ily*;

   prett*y*, prett*ier*, prett*iest*, prett*iness*, prett*ily*

   but gr*ey*, gr*eyer*, gr*eyest*, gr*eyness*, gr*eyly*; c*oy*, c*oyer*, c*oyest*, c*oyness*, c*oyly*

There are, however, exceptions and irregularities for which a dictionary should be consulted.

Words ending in -c

When a suffix beginning with a vowel is added, and the consonant still has a hard *k* sound, *-c* becomes *-ck-*:

picni*c*, picni*ck*ing, picni*ck*ed, picni*ck*er;

mimi*c*, mimi*ck*ing, mimi*ck*ed, mimi*ck*er

-k- is not added in words such as *musician, electricity* etc, where the consonant has the soft sound of *sh* or *s*.

-ie- or -ei-?

i before *e* except after *c*
but only when it rhymes with *tea*
(ie *not* words like height, weight, etc, where the vowel sound
is [*ai*] or [*ei*])

beli*e*f, beli*e*ve, gri*e*f, pi*e*r, si*e*ge;
c*ei*ling, conc*ei*t, dec*ei*t, dec*ei*ve

Exceptions are s*ei*ze, w*ei*rd, and personal names, eg N*ei*l, Sh*ei*la, and place names, eg L*ei*th, Dalk*ei*th, Lake of Ment*ei*th.

The doubling of a final consonant before a following vowel

1. In a word of one syllable, the final consonant is doubled:
   ma*n*, ma*nn*ing, ma*nn*ed, ma*nn*ish;
   re*d*, re*dd*er, re*dd*est, re*dd*en;
   si*n*, si*nn*ing, si*nn*ed, si*nn*er;
   sto*p*, sto*pp*ing, sto*pp*ed, sto*pp*er;
   dru*m*, dru*mm*ing, dru*mm*ed, dru*mm*er
2. In a word of more than one syllable with a short final vowel, the final consonant is doubled only if the accent is on the final syllable:
   entrá*p*, entra*pp*ing, entra*pp*ed;
   regrét, regre*tt*ing, regre*tt*ed;
   begín, begi*nn*ing, begi*nn*er;
   occúr, occu*rr*ing, occu*rr*ed, occu*rr*ence

but   énter, entering, entered;
        prófit, profi*t*ing, profi*t*ed;
        gállop, gallo*p*ing, gallo*p*ed;
        híccup, hiccu*p*ing, hiccu*p*ed
Exceptions are:
   kídnap, kidna*pp*ed, kidna*pp*ing;
   hándicap, handica*pp*ed

3. In British English (but not in AE) *-l* is doubled no matter where the accent falls:
    compél, compelling, compelled;
    trável, travelling, travelled, traveller
4. Some derivatives of words ending in *-s* can be spelt in two ways, eg: bias, biased, biassed.

Words ending with final -e

1. Before a vowel (including *-y*), *-e* is usually dropped:
    come, coming; hate, hating; rage, raging; fame, famous;
    pale, palish; use, usable; ice, icy; noise, noisy; stone, stony
    Some exceptions are intended to distinguish one word from another:
    holey (full of holes), holy;
    dyeing (colouring cloth or hair), dying
2. Before a consonant, *-e* is usually kept:
    hateful, useless, movement, paleness
    Exceptions are:
    true, truly; whole, wholly
    And the final *-e* of judge may be dropped or retained:
    judgment/judgement.
3. *-e* is kept after soft *-c* or *-g* before *-a-*, *-o-*:
    noticeable, traceable, manageable, advantageous

Plural of words ending in -f

It is usual to add *s* to make the plural form, eg:
roof, roofs but there are several exceptions, eg:
calves, elves, knives, wives, leaves.
   Some words have optional spelling, eg:
    hoof, hoofs/hooves
    scarf, scarfs/scarves
    wharf, wharfs/wharves.

The suffix -ful

Take care in spelling adjectives formed by the addition of *-ful*:
    care + full = careful; help + full = helpful

Commonly Misspelt Words/Confusibles

abbreviate
absence (noun) absent (adj)
access/accessible
accidentally
accommodate/accommodation
acknowledge
acquaint/acquaintance
acquire
across
address
advice (noun) advise (verb)
affect (mainly a verb) effect (mainly a noun)
aggravate
aggreeable
amateur
amount
anonymous
answer
anxiety
apology/apologize
apparent
appearance
appreciate/appreciation
architect/architecture
assess
attach
autumn
bachelor
basically
beautiful/beautifully
beginner/beginning
belief (noun) believe (verb)
beneficial/benefited
bolder (adj) eg Harry is *bolder* than Tom.
boulder (noun) eg The men hid behind a big *boulder*.
breadth
Britain (the country) Briton (an inhabitant of Britain)
British
brochure

28

budgeted
bulletin
bureau (pl bureaux/bureaus)
bureaucracy/bureaucratic
business
calendar
career
cashier
category
ceiling
colleague
college
commemorate
commitment
committed/committing
committee
comparative
compatible
competence
conference
connection
connoisseur
conscientious
conscious (adj) eg I was *conscious* during the operation.
conscience (noun) eg James had a guilty *conscience*.
consensus
convenience
correspondence/correspondent
corroborate
courteous
courtesy
curriculum/curriculum vitae
deceive
decide/decision/decisive
deficient
definite
deliberate
dependant (noun) dependent (adj)
dilemma
disappear

disappoint
disapprove
discipline
discreet
discrepancy
dissatisfied
dissimilar
dissolve
distributor
eighth
embarrass/embarrassment
enquire (to ask) inquire (more detailed investigation)
enrol/enrolment *but* enrolled/enrolling
equipment
equipped
especially
etc (etcetera)
exaggeration/exaggerated
excellent
excerpt
excise (cannot be written -ize)
exciting
exercise
exhaust/exhausted/exhaustion
exhibit/exhibition
experience
extraordinary
extremely
favourite
February
financial
finish
foreign/foreigner
forty
fulfil/fulfilled/fulfilment
gauge
government
grammar
grateful
grievance

guarantee
guard
handkerchief (pl handkerchiefs)
harassment
height
honour/honourable – but – honorary
humour – but – humorous
hygiene/hygienic
hypocrisy
hypothesis (pl hypotheses)
immediately
immigrant
imminent
incidentally
incipient
independent
indispensable
influential
install/installation/instalment
intelligence
irrelevant
irreparable
irresistible
its (possessive pronoun) eg The baby played with *its* rattle.
it's (short for *it is*)
jeweller/jewellery (AE jewelry)
judgement/judgment
judicial
knowledge/knowledgeable
language
launderette
leisure
liaison
licence (noun) license (verb)
lose/losing (verb) eg Don't *lose* your purse!
loose (adj) eg These trousers are very *loose*.
lying
maintenance
manoeuvre (AE maneuver)
marriage

Mediterranean
messenger
ministry
miscellaneous
mortgage
necessary
negotiable
neither
niece
ninth
noticeable
nuisance
occasionally
occupation/occupy
occur/occurrence/occurring
offence (noun) offensive (adj)
omit/omitted (verb) omission (noun)
opponent
paid
parallel/paralleled/paralleling
parliament/parliamentary
passenger
permanent
permissible
persevere
personal (adj) eg a *personal* letter
personnel (noun/adj) (staff or employees)
persuade
piece
planning
possess/possessive/possession
potential
practice (noun) practise (verb)
precede/preceding/predecessor
preference/preferred
preliminary
preparation
prestige
privilege
probably

procedure
profession/professional
professor
profit/profitable/profited/profitability
pronunciation
pursue
questionnaire
receipt
receive
recommend/recommendation
reference
refer/referred/referral
repetition
resign/resignation
satisfactory
schedule
scheme
sensible
sentence
separate
similar/similarity/similarly
sincerely
skilful
solicitor
statutory
subtle
subtlety
succeed/success/succession/successful/successfully
suddenness
supersede
suppress
sympathy/sympathetic
tariff
technical
temporary
thorough
transfer/transference/transferred
Tuesday
twelfth
unconscious

undoubtedly
unfortunately
unnecessary
vehicle
warehouse
Wednesday
withhold
wool/woollen/woolly

4

Doing Business:
Enquiries; Offers and Quotations;
Orders; Complaints

The skill needed to write good business letters is exactly the same as is needed for any other written composition. Preparation in the form of notes and a draft will ensure that you include all the points you want to make in a logical order. Use of a dictionary or English usage guide will keep you right as far as vocabulary and grammar are concerned.

Business letters must be brief, to the point and correct. The recipient of a business letter is probably busy so you must get to the point as quickly as possible. Use simple, clear language, avoiding phrases such as 'it seems to be' or 'it may be that'. Always be polite and courteous.

After you have written your letter read it carefully, checking punctuation and spelling. Make certain that the recipient will understand exactly what you mean to say. If anything is unclear, write the letter again. It is quicker to do this than to write a second letter at a later date to clear up a point which has been misunderstood.

Form and Layout of a Business Letter
Letters should be typed on the company letterhead in single-line spacing, unless they are very short, when double-line spacing can be used.

The most widely used and economical layout for a business letter is the fully blocked style with 'open' punctuation. All the parts of the letter are set against the left-hand margin which should be aligned with the firm's printed letterheading. No punctuation is used except to ensure clarity in the address and the text of the letter. Abbreviations do not need full stops.

1. *D E A N S   B O O K S*

    8 Dukery Gate
    London
    SW2P 4YX

    Director: Michael C Dean

    Tel 031 557 4571

2. Ref: DT/HS

3. 21 April 1991

4. Bertram Schultz
    Medical Book Shop
    Siegesdenkmal
    7800 FREIBURG
    Germany

5. Attention: Ms Helmtraud Schultz

6. Dear Ms Schultz

7. DEANS MEDICAL DICTIONARY

8. Thank you for your letter of 18 April asking for an advance
    copy of our above publication to be released shortly.

    I am sending you a copy under separate cover along with our
    advertising material and 1991 catalogue. As you will see, we
    have widened our range to include popular psychology and
    esoteric books.

    If you have any questions or would like more information on
    any of our publications, please do not hesitate to get in
    touch. I look forward to hearing from you soon.

9. Yours sincerely

    Doris Tate

10. Doris Tate
11. Export Manager

1. *Printed letterhead* – gives all the necessary information about the company:

   ● registered name
   ● registered office
   ● logo (if any)
   ● list of names of directors, company officials or principals
   ● branch offices and/or subsidiary companies (if any)
   ● telephone number(s) and STD code
   ● telex and/or fax number (if any)
   ● VAT number (if any)

   The modern tendency is for the printed letterhead to be blocked to the left-hand margin so as to then match the fully blocked letter layout.

2. *References* – initials and/or numbers may be used. The addressee's reference (if any) usually comes first. References may also be placed at the bottom of the letter, usually above 'Enc'. (See 13.)

3. *Date* – following the order day, month, year. American writers sometimes put the month first, so you need to watch out for this.

4. *Inside Address* – the address of the recipient. It should be exactly the same as the address shown on the envelope.

   When writing to a man, his name should appear as 'Mr A. Smith'. If you are writing to a woman, use the title 'Ms' unless you are aware of a clear preference for 'Mrs' or 'Miss'. Titles like 'Dr', 'Professor' etc should be used when appropriate. One title only is used in English – do not write * Professor Dr Jones or * Dr Mrs Smith.

   If you do not know the name of a particular person in a company or organization, but you know the person's position, you may address your letter to 'The Manager', 'The Secretary', 'The Director', etc.

   If you know neither the name nor the position of the person who will read your letter, you should address your letter directly to the company concerned, eg: 'Smith and Wesson Ltd', 'Richards &

Co'. ('Ltd' and 'Co' are the usual abbreviations for 'Limited' and 'Company'.)

5. *Attention line* – (optional).
6. *Salutation* – see *Note 1*.
7. *Subject line*.
8. *Body of the letter* – a business letter usually has three main parts:

- introduction;
- development;
- conclusion.

9. *Complimentary close* – see *Note 1*.
10. *Signature* – see *Note 2*.
11. *Name and position of the writer*.
12. *Carbon copies* (optional).
13. *Enc(s)/Encl(s)/Enclosure(s)* – (optional).

Note 1: Salutations/complimentary closes

The usual salutation and complimentary close for British business letters is '*Dear Sir(s)/Madam*' followed by '*Yours faithfully*' or '*Dear Mr/Mrs/Miss/Ms*' followed by '*Yours sincerely*'. American business letters use the salutation '*Gentlemen*' followed by '*Very truly yours*'.

Dear Sir	**Dear Mr Brown**	**Gentlemen**
Yours faithfully	**Yours sincerely**	**Very truly yours**

Note 2: Signature

A signature may be prefaced by the abbreviation '*pp*', meaning 'per pro' – for and on behalf of – when the letter has been signed by someone else on behalf of the sender.

Yours sincerely

Sarah Jones

pp Doris Tate
Export Manager

Continuation sheet

A business letter should be concise and, where possible, extend to no more than one page. The word content therefore needs to be limited to around three hundred words (excluding the address, salutation, etc). If a letter is longer than this, a continuation sheet is used. This is usually plain paper with no letterhead, though sometimes carrying the firm's logo. It should be of the same quality as the top sheet. Details of page number, date and addressee's name are given at the top of the page against the left-hand margin.

The continuation sheet must contain at least one full sentence and, preferably, a whole paragraph. If 'Yours sincerely' and a signature are the only things appearing on page two, your letter will look badly planned, and must be redrafted.

2

7 July 1991

Mr Henry Ross

I will get the plans off to you as soon as possible and look forward to hearing your remarks about them when we meet in August.

Yours sincerely

Ian Davidson

Ian Davidson
Group Manager

Encs

Compliment Slips

Compliment slips are used to accompany leaflets and small items where a letter is not considered necessary. They are usually small pieces of paper (eg ⅓ A4 size = 210 × 99 mm) which have details of the firm and *With Compliments* printed on them. The details are the same as those printed on the firm's letterhead.

Memoranda

Commonly called '*memos*', these are written messages sent between employees within the same organization, ie in the same building, or to representatives or agents based elsewhere in the country or abroad.

Printed memo forms are often used, specifying: From; To; Date; Reference (of originator); Subject and Topic if different topics are being dealt with. Leave one line space between a heading and the text.

If writing a memo on a plain sheet of plain paper, leave a good margin all round the message. At least 2.5cm *all* the way round is recommended.

No formal salutation or complimentary close is used. If there is an enclosure (or enclosures), Enc(s) should be marked at the end of the memo, against the left-hand margin. A copy of the memo should be retained for filing.

If your memo is handwritten, make sure that everything is legible.

M E M O R A N D U M

To: All members of staff

From: The Personnel Manager

Date: 12 June 1991

Ref: MP

SMOKING

Members of staff are reminded that the canteen is a NO SMOKING AREA and that smoking is restricted to the coffee lounge and terrace.

BICYCLES

Members of staff who cycle to work should leave their bicycles behind the boilerhouse until further notice.

Composing Business Letters

A good business letter should be concise, courteous and correct in tone. It should generally consist of three parts as follows:

1. *Introduction* (one paragraph) – states the subject of the letter, acknowledges a correspondent's letter if one has been received, quoting its date and reference, if any.
2. *Development* (one or more paragraphs) – deals in a methodical way with the subject previously referred to in the introduction, ie lists facts or arguments, gives detailed explanation, outlines a course of action.
3. *Conclusion* (one paragraph) – usually kept for expressions of goodwill, intended to leave a favourable impression in the reader's mind.

However, the exact composition of any letter will naturally depend on the purpose for which you are writing.

The use of subject or topic headings, especially in a complicated matter, helps the letter to be correctly routed, gains the reader's interest and saves time.

Be specific and give full details, eg relevant dates, prices and descriptions of articles, specification numbers and components. Consider the letter from the reader's standpoint: what the writer takes for granted may not be obvious to the person receiving the letter. Check that all the correspondent's queries have been answered.

Avoid opening the final sentence with a present participle like hoping, trusting, wishing, eg * 'Thanking you for your prompt attention to our order . . .' The plain statement 'We thank you for your prompt attention to our order' is preferable.

Remember, good business letters help to create good public relations. The tone of a letter reveals the writer's personality; a co-operative person writes a friendly constructive letter which will do its job much better than a rude letter. Courtesy is more than the occasional use of a polite word or phrase. The reader's response should be constantly borne in mind and tactful phrasing sought:

'As we do not appear to have received . . .' is friendlier than * 'As you forgot to enclose . . .'

'May I clear up some points . . .' will be better accepted than * 'You appear to have misunderstood several points'.

Enquiries

For a *simple enquiry*, a postcard stating the nature of the enquiry and giving your address and the date is all that is needed.

25 Lansdown Street
Mantown
M11 7BT

25/2/91

Dear Sir/Madam

Please send details of your D.I.Y. picture frame kits as advertised in the Sunday Post.

Yours faithfully

Raymond Smith

If you need a lot of information or want to give details of your needs, write a *letter of enquiry*. You may want to ask about some or all of the following:

- description of the goods in as much detail as possible;
- supply of goods;
- availability of the goods and delivery time;
- leaflets, catalogues, brochures;
- patterns, samples;
- prices, quotations; if you are limited to a certain price range, mention it;
- terms of payment, method of delivery and insurance.

Common terms relating to prices are:

- *B/E – bill of exchange;*

- *ex-works/ex-factory* – the price from the place of origin of the goods; the buyer pays for transport;
- *FOB (free on board)* – the price includes delivery to a named port and loading on to a ship (eg FOB Hull);
- *CIF (cost, insurance, freight)* – the price includes all costs and insurance to a named destination (eg CIF Manchester);
- *COD – cash on delivery.*

If you are *writing to a supplier for the first time* include the following points:

- where you found the supplier's name;
- information about your business;
- where the supplier can ask for references about your firm.

If you have made personal contact with a representative, you should write to him directly. If you do not know anyone personally, write to the Sales Manager, starting your letter with 'Dear Sir/Madam'.

When writing on behalf of your firm use 'we' throughout. If writing as an individual, use 'I', 'me', etc.

Letter of enquiry from a retailer to a manufacturer

Dear Sir/Madam

We saw your leather goods at the London Leather Trade Fair in August this year and we are sure that your handbags, purses and briefcases would find a ready market in our part of the country.

Our shop is in the centre of Oxford and is used not only by members of the university, both staff and students, but also by the many tourists who visit the city throughout the year. We carry a fairly large stock and we are always in need of supplies from quality manufacturers like yourselves.

(cont. overleaf)

Would you kindly send us your current catalogue and price list. If your prices are competitive, you can count on regular and substantial orders from us. We shall, of course, supply the usual trade references if we order from you.

We look forward to hearing from you soon.

Yours faithfully

Export enquiry

Dear Sir/Madam

Our agents in Germany have asked us for quotations for 10 000 jars of marmalade to be sold in a 'Best of Britain' week in a big department store chain throughout Germany.

Please let us know what quantities you can deliver and quote your best terms CIF Hamburg.

Yours faithfully

Asking for goods on approval

Dear Mr Simpson

Thank you for your last delivery of desk lamps. You will be pleased to hear that they are selling well.

As you know, we have been thinking for some time about expanding our business and selling larger items of office furniture such as desks and chairs. I see from your latest catalogue that you have two very reasonably priced swivel chairs, catalogue numbers SW 34 and SW 38. I should be very pleased if you would let me have three of each of the above on approval to see if they find a response with my customers.

In anticipation of your agreeing to this, I look forward to taking delivery of the chairs in the near future.

Yours sincerely

Asking for information

> Dear Mr Smith
>
> I read in yesterday's *Evening Post* that you are now taking applications from exhibitors for the 1991 May Fair. I should be grateful if you would send me details of the fair including the current prices per square metre for stands and the latest date for submitting an application.
>
> Yours sincerely

Useful phrases

Opening phrases
We were given your name by . . .
You have been recommended to us by . . .
Your articles have been recommended to us by . . .
. . . has been kind enough to give us your address.
As we have learned from . . . you are manufacturers of . . .
We saw your advertisement in the current issue of . . .
We have heard that you have put a new . . . on the market.
We saw your stand at a recent trade fair.
We visited your stand at the . . . exhibition.
We refer to your special offer of . . .

Reasons for enquiring
We are a subsidiary of . . .
We are a . . . company based in . . .
We are a company specializing in . . .
We are interested in . . .
We sell/need/are in the market for . . .
We have received many enquiries from our customers for . . .
Our stocks of . . . are running low.
We would like to expand our range of . . .

Asking for price lists, catalogues, etc
I should be grateful if you would send me . . .
Please send your current/latest catalogue/price list/brochure.
We would like you to send us some samples/patterns.
Please send us full details about your products.
Please quote your prices for these articles/goods/products.

Please quote your best/most competitive/lowest prices.

Please quote your prices gross/net/FOB.

We would like to know if you are prepared to grant
  discounts.

Please let us know the minimum quantity for a trial order.

We should appreciate further details/information about
  (your) . . .

Please send further details/information about (your) . . .

Please include information about packing and shipping.

We should like to know your earliest date of delivery.

What would be your earliest delivery date?

Please let us know on what terms you can deliver.

Please let us know if you can supply from stock.

Please let me know your terms of business.

We would find it most helpful if your representative could
  call on us.

Giving references

Information about our company can be got from . . .

For information about our company please refer to/write
  to/contact . . .

Should you wish to make any enquiries about us, please refer
  to/write to/contact . . .

. . . will be glad to give you information about us.

We shall be pleased to provide the usual trade references.

First-class British and French references can be provided.

Future business

If the goods come up to our expectations . . .

If the samples meet with our approval . . .

If your prices are competitive and your goods up to standard
  . . .

If terms and delivery date are satisfactory . . .

  . . . I/we would expect to place regular orders.

  . . . I/we intend to place substantial orders.

  . . . I/we shall order on a regular basis.

  . . . you can expect regular orders.

Closing phrases

I/We hope to hear from you in the near future.

I/We look forward to hearing from you soon.
I/We would be pleased to hear from you soon.
A prompt reply/an early reply would be appreciated.

Replying to Enquiries; Offers, Unsolicited Offers

A reply to an enquiry may take the form of a simple quotation, containing only the prices and other information asked for. Many people, however, take the opportunity to stimulate a customer's interest in the goods or services asked about and write a letter. When *replying to an enquiry by letter*:

- thank the writer for the enquiry, citing the date of the enquiry letter in the first instance;
- quote a reference number if there is one;
- make sure that all the enquiries have been answered;
- let the prospective customer know if the goods are available immediately or, if not, how long any delay may be; if you do not have the goods requested, offer an alternative if possible;
- mention one or two selling points like guarantees or after-sales services;
- enclose current price lists, catalogues or leaflets and inform the customer of other items in stock that may be of interest;
- show willingness to supply further information; if a demonstration is necessary, offer it;
- give as many details as possible about prices, stating your terms of business and delivery charges.

A *firm offer* is subject to certain conditions, such as a deadline for the receipt of orders or a discount for certain quantities or prompt payment. Do not forget to mention these points.

Unsolicited offers can be sent to prospective customers who have not made an enquiry. These offers try to sell a product and should include all the information which will encourage a prospective customer to buy. Unsolicited offers can be sent as *circulars*, in which case they require no inside address, formal salutation or complimentary close. However, a better response will result if an unsolicited offer is written in the form of a letter.

Follow this scheme:

- start the letter by telling the recipient where you found his or her name;
- describe your firm and what you have to offer;
- give a detailed description of the goods, emphasizing the selling points;
- state prices, and discounts if any;
- state the terms of delivery and payment and specify delivery times;
- if you are offering a product to a customer who has not placed an order with you for some time, ask why this has happened.

Quotation

> Dear Sir/Madam
>
> Thank you for your letter of 22 June, asking for a quotation for 100 mixers. We are pleased to make the following offer:
>
> Price: Ex-works: £62.50 each
> Packing: Free
> Payment: 30 days net
> Delivery: 7 days after receipt of order.
>
> We look forward to receiving your order and assure you that it will receive our prompt attention.
>
> Yours faithfully

Reply to the letter of enquiry on page 43

> Dear Sir/Madam
>
> Many thanks for your enquiry of 3 September regarding the handbags, purses and briefcases which you saw at the Leather Trade Fair. All the models which were on

(cont. on next page)

display there are available and can be delivered to you from stock by the beginning of November, subject to receiving your firm order by 15 September.

We enclose our current catalogue and price list and ask you to quote catalogue numbers and colours when ordering. As we have not done business before, we would prefer payment COD.

If this offer is acceptable to you, please let us have your order as soon as possible. We can assure you that it will be dealt with promptly.

Yours faithfully

Reply to an enquiry for samples

Dear Ms Roberts

Thank you for your enquiry of 25 March asking for samples of our different cotton weights. We enclose these together with a pattern card showing the various colours and patterns available in the different weights.

Our delivery date is approximately two weeks from receipt of order except for our 'Madras' cotton which takes up to six weeks, depending on the season.

All our prices are quoted CIF Liverpool. We offer a discount of 10% for payment within one calendar month.

We hope that our samples meet your approval and look forward to hearing from you soon.

Yours sincerely

Circular

We have received so many enquiries in the last few months for our 'Antique' table lamps that we feel sure that you will be interested in them too.

(cont. overleaf)

These electric lamps are made to the highest standard in best quality metal and are exact replicas of Victorian oil lamps. Unlike the old lamps, however, they are easily maintained because their 'brass-look' finish needs no polishing or cleaning. Each lamp comes with a plain glass inner funnel and an etched glass lampshade in white, pink or orange.

We enclose our catalogue and price list from which you can see that we offer very good terms for large orders.

We are sure that these lamps will find a ready market in your area and look forward to receiving your order soon.

Unsolicited offer

Dear Sir/Madam

We have seen your name in various trade magazines and note that you are one the leading importers of oriental herbs and spices. As export agents for the Chilli Spice Company, we feel sure that we can make you a very favourable offer.

We enclose our latest catalogue and price list which will give you full information about our wide range of herbs and spices.

Our prices are stated CIF Hull and include packing. Shipment can be effected within one week of receipt of order. Our terms are payment by irrevocable letter of credit opened through the Santander Bank, Manila.

We are sure that our varied range and competitive prices will encourage you to place an order with us. We look forward to the pleasure of doing business with you.

Yours faithfully

An offer to an old customer

> Dear Mr Michaelson
>
> I am writing to call your attention to our new range of hand-embroidered pillowcases which I am sure will interest you and your customers. As you can see from the enclosed sample, the embroidery is expertly done on 100% cotton which is of our usual high quality.
>
> On looking over our records, I see that you have not placed an order with us for the last four months. If this is due to any difficulties which I can help you with, I will be more than pleased to do so.
>
> I look forward to hearing from you soon.
>
> Yours sincerely

Useful phrases

Opening phrases

We thank you for your enquiry of . . .

Many thanks for your enquiry of . . .

Thank you for your enquiry of . . .

In reply to your enquiry of . . .

    . . . we have pleasure in offering you the following: . . ./

    . . . we enclose our estimate/quotation for the supply of . . ./

    . . . we are sending you . . .

We were pleased to note from your letter of . . . that you are interested in . . .

We think you may be interested in . . .

I am writing to call your attention to our new . . .

We have had so many enquiries recently for our . . .

We have seen your name in various trade magazines . . .

The product

We have a wide selection of . . .

We have recently put a new . . . on the market.

The goods you ask for are/are not in stock.

We hope that the goods will suit you.

Catalogues, brochures, etc

Please find enclosed our latest catalogue / brochure / price list.

We are sending you our latest . . .

The enclosed illustrated leaflet will give you an idea of our range of . . .

We enclose our latest catalogue and price list which will give you full information about our range of . . .

Prices, terms of payment and delivery

Our prices include postage and packing.

Please add . . . for postage and packing.

The prices are stated/quoted . . . and include packing.

We would like to call your attention to the special conditions.

Our prices are ex-works.

The prices quoted in the attached price list are ex-works.

The prices are subject to change.

Prices are likely to rise soon.

Our usual terms are COD.

Payment should be made with a B/E.

We would like payment by irrevocable and confirmed letter of credit.

Our terms are payment by irrevocable letter of credit opened through the . . . Bank.

We offer quantity discounts on orders over . . .

A . . .% discount is offered on payment within . . . weeks.

Our prices compare favourably with those of our competitors.

The goods can be delivered immediately/from stock.

Delivery will be effected as soon as possible.

Shipment can be effected within . . . of receipt of goods.

Our delivery date is approximately . . . after receipt of your order.

If you order by . . . we can assure you of delivery by . . .

We cannot promise delivery within the period stated in your enquiry.

Closing phrases

We feel that our wide selection of . . . will appeal to your customers.

We would like to thank you for your interest in our products
. . .
We hope that the enclosed samples will meet with your
    approval . . .
We know that you have made an excellent choice in selecting
    this model/product . . .
    . . . and can assure you that your order will be dealt with
        promptly/
    . . . and hope that you can make use of this offer/
    . . . and feel sure that we can make you a very favourable
        offer/
We are sure that our varied range and competitive prices will
    encourage you to place an order with us.
If you have any further questions, please do not hesitate to
    write or telephone us.
We hope that our favourable prices will induce you to place
    an order.
I/We look forward to your instructions by return.
I/We hope to hear from you in the near future.

Orders, Counter-Offers, Cancellations

Orders are placed either on the buyer's own initiative or in response to an offer. If an offer suits him, the buyer simply places an order, often using a printed order form. However, if there is no order form or certain points have to be discussed, then a letter is needed. Sometimes a *counter-offer* is written in order to try to get a concession from the seller.

The buyer is entitled to *cancel* his order at any time before it has been accepted by the seller. If the order has been accepted, and the buyer must cancel for some reason, then the matter has to be discussed. Needless to say, if the seller fails to perform his duty, then the buyer may cancel at any time.

When writing an *order*:

- thank the seller for the offer or say where you have seen his goods offered;
- if there is an order number, use it;
- if there is no order number, give a full description of the goods you want;

- state the number of items you wish to order;
- state the price and method of payment.

If you are writing a *counter-offer*:

- give your reasons for rejecting the first offer politely;
- make your counter-offer clear and firm;
- if possible, offer to pay something on account;
- end the letter with a polite request for a reply to your counter-offer.

If you have difficulties and are forced to make a *cancellation* after an order has been accepted by the seller:

- begin the letter by apologizing for the cancellation;
- politely give your reasons for cancelling;
- reassure the seller that there will be other opportunities to do business in the future.

If you are cancelling an order because the seller has failed to perform his duty:

- give details of the goods;
- state the reasons for the cancellation;
- tell the seller that you are unhappy or dissatisfied with his behaviour;
- be polite.

Order for bunk beds

Dear Sir/Madam

With reference to your advertisement in the *Evening Herald* for bunk beds I would like to order one set. I enclose a cheque for £120 to cover the cost of the beds and delivery to the above address.

Yours faithfully

Order for computer

Dear Sir/Madam

Please supply the following:

One (1) Pyramid Computer as per your quotation of 24 November

Price: £3500 including delivery

We note from your quotation that you can deliver from stock and will expect the computer within the next fortnight.

Yours faithfully

Counter-offer

Dear Sir/Madam

Thank you for your letter of 5 March enclosing your brochure and price list.

We have noted that your varnish is made to the highest environmental standards and we are sure that this will be a good selling point here. However, there is one disadvantage when comparing your prices to those of other manufacturers. Most firms in the EC are now packaging in one-litre tins. Since your varnish is packed in pint tins, we feel that customers will suspect that they are not getting their money's worth. Because of this, we ask you to reduce the prices quoted by 10%.

If you are prepared to do this, we should like to buy 10 000 tins: 5000 tins matt and 5000 tins high gloss. On our side, we would be willing to pay 50% of the total invoice on receipt of the goods.

Please let us know as soon as possible if you can supply us on the terms quoted.

Yours faithfully

Cancellation of order due to unforeseen circumstances

Dear Sir/Madam

We regret having to cancel our order No 1237 HU of 24 November 1990.

The roof of our High Street branch was so badly damaged during a recent storm that the premises were flooded. It is impossible for us to do business at the moment. As we have no storage space for the goods, we see no alternative but to cancel our order.

Our builders estimate that repairs will take at least six months. We hope to be able to place another order then and are sure that we can make up for this inconvenience to you.

Yours faithfully

Cancellation of order due to delay in delivery

Dear Mr King

Order NMP 66579

The long delay in the execution of this order has caused us a great deal of worry. We stated clearly in our order that the goods must reach us no later than 31 March but, in spite of repeated letters and telephone conversations, they have still not arrived. This delay in delivery puts us in a very difficult position as we have customers waiting for the goods.

You will understand that we are very unhappy about this state of affairs and can see no alternative but to cancel the order.

Yours faithfully

Useful phrases

Opening Phrases

Thank you for your offer of . . .

I/We have examined your circular with interest . . .

Please find enclosed order form No . . .

I/We would like to order the following: . . .

Please accept the following order for . . .

We are particularly interested in . . .

Please send me the following articles/goods: . . .

Payment will be made on receipt of the goods/within 30
    days/on the terms agreed.

Counter-offers

We cannot accept your offer because . . .
    . . . your prices are too high/
    . . . local competition is too fierce.

Could you consider reducing your prices by . . .?

If you can reduce your prices by . . .

If you can meet our wishes regarding the price . . .

Cancellations

We regret having to cancel our order for . . .

We are sorry to have to inform you that we must cancel our
    order for . . .

We reserve the right to cancel the order.

The goods are not up to standard/of inferior quality/do not
    match up to samples.

We hope to be able to place another order soon.

We stated in our order that the goods must reach us by . . . at
    the latest.

Your delay in delivery puts us in a very difficult/
    embarrassing position.

Closing phrases

Your careful attention to our instructions will be appreciated.

We hope that you can give this order your prompt and
    careful attention.

We expect your answer by return of post.

We shall hold you liable for any losses.

We can see no alternative but to cancel this order.

Complaints
Making a complaint

When things go wrong, when equipment does not work, when an order is late or when goods arrive damaged, it is necessary to write a letter of complaint. Theoretically you should write a letter of complaint as soon as a defect or deficiency becomes apparent. However, in order to ensure that your complaint is dealt with the minimum of fuss, you must state the facts coolly and clearly. This is difficult to do if you are angry or frustrated so *never write a letter of complaint in the heat of the moment*. By all means note down your reasons for complaint, but leave these notes to one side for a while, and write the letter later.

Stick to the following rules:

- if you do not know the name of the person responsible for dealing with complaints, address your letter to *Customer Complaints Department*;
- make the subject of the letter clear from the start; if there is an order number, or some other means of identification, place it at the beginning of the letter;
- set out the facts of the case, giving concrete examples or explanations;
- make sure that you have got your facts right;
- make definite suggestions about what is to be done;
- if you have to send documents of any kind, send copies, not the originals;
- be firm but friendly, tactful and polite; you are in the right and have no need to be rude.

Goods not received

Dear Sir/Madam

No CDTEM 023

On 26 July I ordered the above-mentioned CD from your catalogue, enclosing a cheque for £8.95. A recent bank statement shows that my cheque was presented for payment on 2 August but, to date, I have not received the CD.

(cont. on next page)

As a relatively long period of time has now elapsed, and I have heard nothing from you about a delay in delivery, I assume that the CD has gone astray in the post.

Please look into this matter and let me know as soon as possible when I can expect the CD to arrive.

Yours faithfully

Asking for a price reduction

Dear Sir/Madam

Wilton carpeting. Delivery note No 34, dated 21/3/90

We were pleased to take delivery of the above carpeting last week. Unfortunately, on comparing it with the sample which you originally sent us, we found that the pattern is not exactly the same. The sample is brown with beige spots but the carpeting which was delivered has orange spots. However, as we can see that the quality is the same, we are prepared to accept the brown and orange carpeting.

None the less, we feel that we are entitled to some sort of compensation and would suggest a 5% discount on the price per square metre. If you agree, please let us know as soon as possible.

We look forward to hearing from you soon.

Yours faithfully

A complaint about damaged goods

Dear Sir/Madam

The box of twenty-four TMS video cassettes, order number BBG 134, which we ordered from you on 6 June, arrived yesterday.

We are sorry to inform you that when we opened the box we found that the top layer of cassettes, six in all, were

(cont. overleaf)

damaged. The plastic outer covers on all six cassettes are cracked and two of the videos have been so badly damaged that they are unplayable.

As this seems to have been due to bad packaging on your part, we are returning the damaged cassettes at your expense. We look forward to receiving six replacement video cassettes as soon as possible.

Yours faithfully

Useful phrases

Opening phrases explaining the problem

We are sorry to tell you that your last delivery has given us cause for complaint.

Part of the consignment/order No. ... was damaged in transit/during transport.

The damage seems to be due to/to have been caused by ... faulty/bad/inadequate packing.

Under the terms of your guarantee ...

We are returning the goods to you ...

We cannot accept these goods ...

Making suggestions about what can be done

We are prepared to accept the goods if you reduce the price by .../if you grant us a reduction of ...

Please exchange the faulty items ...

Please send me a refund ...

Please send us replacements for the damaged/faulty goods as soon as possible.

I am returning the goods at your expense for credit.

We are placing the faulty goods at your disposal.

Closing phrases

This has caused me a great deal of annoyance/inconvenience/embarrassment.

Please let me know what you intend to do.

I hope you will look into this matter as soon as possible.

We shall expect you to be more careful in the future.

We hope that this will not happen again.

Replying to Complaints

If a complaint is received, look into the matter as quickly as possible. If you cannot make a decision promptly, send a brief acknowledgment, telling the complainant that the problem is receiving attention. Always try to deal with the complaint to the complainant's satisfaction if he is in the right; if there is no fault on your side but the complainant feels he is justified (ie makes a *mistaken complaint*), try to suggest a compromise. *Unfounded complaints* are, of course, always rejected, but even in this case a reply is necessary. It goes without saying that replies to unfounded complaints should be polite.

In the case of *justified complaints*:

- admit your mistake and apologize to the complainant;
- suggest a way of putting things right;
- reassure the complainant that the same mistake will not happen again;
- express the hope that business relations will continue.

Some firms make a practice of sending a complainant a small gift, often a new product which they will hope will encourage future orders.

When replying to a *mistaken complaint*:

- express regret that the complainant feels there is cause for complaint;
- point out tactfully that the complaint is not justified and explain why;
- suggest a compromise, if appropriate.

An *unfounded complaint* should be treated in the same polite way as a mistaken complaint though no compromise should be suggested.

Dear Mr James

6 × TMS Video Cassettes, part of order number
BBG 134

I refer to your letter of 23 June which arrived this morning together with the above-mentioned damaged video cassettes.

I am very sorry that you had to go to the trouble of returning the cassettes. I have checked them and agree with you that the damage must have been due to bad packing. Though our warehouse staff are trained to pack all our goods carefully, it is obvious that your consignment was not packed to our usual high standards. I can assure you that this will not happen again.

Six replacement videos have been sent off to you this morning, together with six of our new TMA Audio Cassettes which I hope you will accept as a gift.

Once again, please accept my sincere apologies. I look forward to our continued good business relations.

Yours sincerely

Rejecting a complaint

Dear Mr North

Magic Paint Stripper

Thank you for your letter of 10 March regarding the state of the fibre-glass hull of your boat after being treated with our paint stripper.

While we are very sorry that this unfortunate accident has occurred, we should like to point out that Magic

(cont. on next page)

Paint Stripper is *only* to be used on wood or metal surfaces. It states very clearly, not only on the tin, but also in the accompanying instruction leaflet, that Magic Paint Stripper should never be used on plastic, fibre-glass or other man-made materials.

I am sure that you will agree that, under the circumstances, we cannot grant your claim.

Yours faithfully

Useful phrases

Opening phrases
Thank you for writing to us about . . .
We apologize for our mistake . . .

Making suggestions about what can be done
We are prepared to exchange the goods.
The faulty items will be exchanged.
A new consignment is being sent off to you today.
Enclosed you will find our cheque/credit note for . . . representing a refund on the goods you returned to us.
We are anxious to settle the matter to your entire satisfaction.
Please return the goods at our expense for credit.

Closing phrases
Please accept our apologies for the trouble you have been caused.
We hope that we can continue with our good business relationship in the future.
We would like to assure you that the mistake will not happen again.
We will make every effort to ensure that the mistake does not occur again.
We hope that you agree with/approve of the arrangement we have suggested.

Rejecting complaints

You will agree that under the circumstances we cannot accept/agree to the return of the goods.

We cannot assume any liability in this case.

We are confident that the machine will give satisfactory results if you follow the operating instructions.

We would suggest that you report the damage to your insurance company.

5

Employment:
Applications and CVs; Letters of Confirmation, Acceptance and Resignation; References and Testimonials

Applications and CVs

Great care should be taken when writing a *letter of application* for a job. If there are a lot of applicants a good letter can get you an interview whereas a bad letter will simply be ignored.

Some applicants make the mistake of phrasing their letter in an unusual way. Others write on purple paper, thinking that this will make their application stand out. A straightforward letter on good quality notepaper will give a much more favourable impression. Unless your handwriting is quite illegible an application should usually be handwritten. Do not use coloured ink. Black or dark blue is best and a fountain pen looks better than Biro.

Many advertisements ask applicants to write a brief letter and send a *curriculum vitae* (cv) or personal data sheet (AE). This should set out neatly, on one sheet of paper, details about the applicant, his or her education, training and experience. Unless otherwise stated, a cv or personal data sheet should be typed. When submitting a cv, try to bring one or two relevant skills or qualifications into your covering letter.

In many EC countries and in the United States it is the custom to enclose a recent photograph with an application.

When *replying to an advertisement for a position*:

● write from your home address;

- say where you saw the advertisement or heard about the position;
- say why you are applying for that particular post;
- state your qualifications and offer copies of relevant certificates;
- if you are working, describe what you are doing now and give reasons why you want to change your job.

If no post has been advertised but you know of a vacancy, or think you may have a chance of employment sometime in the future, you can write an *unsolicited application*:

When writing an unsolicited application:

- address the person responsible for the position by name when possible;
- mention the mutual contact or acquaintance who told you that there might be a vacancy;
- include any other points mentioned above which may be relevant.

Curriculum vitae – CV

CURRICULUM VITAE

Personal details:	David Brown, 21 South Road, Richmond, Surrey RD7 6AJ
Date of birth:	16 March 1967
Place of birth:	Richmond, Surrey
Parents:	Thomas Brown, businessman Edith Brown, art teacher
Marital status:	Single
Education:	Richmond Primary School
	Richmond Senior School

(cont. on next page)

GCE O level mathematics,
French, German, art.

GCE A level German, French,
art.

Business experience:
2 years' employment in the Richmond Antiques Mart.

Special qualifications:
I am currently attending an evening course in Marketing and Sales at the Richmond Business School and have passed the intermediate examination with Credit.

Letter in reply to an advertisement

Dear Sir/Madam

Trainee Auctioneer

With reference to your advertisement in today's *Times*, I would like to be considered for the above-mentioned post.

My present position is in an antiques market where I have special responsibility for Victorian furniture and paintings. I feel, however, that I would like to specialize in porcelain and china.

Since the age of fifteen I have been a keen student of antiques, learning more and more through the years. I am also an enthusiastic collector of Meissen and Hutchenreuter porcelain.

I would be very pleased if I could find employment in such a famous house as yours.

I enclose a curriculum vitae and a recent photograph. I hope to hear from you soon.

Yours faithfully

Encs: Curriculum vitae
        Photograph

Unsolicited application

Dear Mr Donaldson

I have heard from Mr Richardson, chief technician in the Haematology Department at Leeds General Infirmary, that you are looking for laboratory technicians for your company.

After leaving school in 1967, I trained as a laboratory technician at the Leeds General Infirmary. I attended day release classes and evening school and qualified as a medical laboratory technician (IMLT) in 1972. I continued to work at the Leeds General Infirmary until 1976 when I moved into research at Parson's Homeopathic Ltd. I have been there until now.

Unfortunately, due to the closure of Parson's I have to find new employment. As I would like to stay in the research field and especially in homeopathic medicine, I would like to apply for a post with your company.

My chief of staff, Mr Graham, will be pleased to give you any information you want about my work. I can make myself available for an interview at your convenience.

Yours sincerely

Useful phrases

Opening phrases

In reply to/With reference to your advertisement in . . . of . . . I would like to apply for the position of . . . in your company.

I see from your advertisement in . . . that you are looking for a . . .

I recently heard from . . . that there is a vacancy in your . . . department.

. . . of . . . has told me that some time in May there will be a vacancy/an opening for . . . in your office.

Education/work experience

I attended . . . school for . . . years.
In 19. . . I graduated from . . .
I enrolled for a year's course at . . .
I studied . . .
I have a degree in . . . from the University of . . .
During training for my present job I attended classes in . . .
I have trained as a . . .
I served my apprenticeship at . . .
    . . . and am thoroughly familiar with all aspects of office
    work/export procedure/trade.
I have had . . . years' experience in . . .
I speak fluent Spanish.
I speak French and German fluently.
My proficiency in Italian means that I would be able to
    handle all the Italian correspondence on my own.

Reasons for wanting a change

I would like the opportunity to work on my own initiative/
    with children/with old people.
My reason for applying for the post is that I would like to
    have more responsibility.
My reason for looking for a change is the better opportunities
    offered by a large company like yours.
My present employer is closing down his business.
As my family is moving to . . . I am looking for employment
    there.

Closing phrases

Please refer to the enclosed curriculum vitae/personal data
    sheet for further particulars.
For information about my character/work record, please
    contact . . .
I hope I may be granted an interview, when I can explain
    my qualifications in more detail.

Confirming an Offer of Employment

If you have offered someone a position and they have
accepted it, it is customary to write a letter *confirming
employment*. The letter should:

- state the position being offered;
- confirm the date and starting time of the first day of work;
- mention any documents which the new employee should send or bring with him/her;
- offer help in case of any misunderstandings about working conditions;
- end by saying something positive about the new working relationship.

Confirming employment

Dear Mr Forbes

With reference to our telephone conversation of this morning I am pleased to confirm the offer of a position as a salesman with our company, starting on 1 March 1990.

I enclose information about our pension scheme and other fringe benefits as well as two copies of your contract of employment. Please sign one copy of the contract and return it to me as soon as possible. If you have any questions about your conditions of employment, please do not hesitate to get in touch.

I look forward to welcoming you in our High Street offices at 9.30 am on 1 March and hope this will be the beginning of a long and mutually beneficial association.

Yours sincerely

Accepting a Position

Many employers do not expect a *letter of acceptance* if a position has been offered and accepted verbally. However, if written confirmation of acceptance is asked for:

- thank the employer for the offer of employment;
- accept the post;
- enclose any contracts or other papers which you have been asked for;
- confirm that you will be there on the starting date.

Acceptance

> Dear Ms Hall
>
> Thank you very much for your letter of 6 January offering me the position of salesman with your company. I will be very pleased to start work with your company on 1 March 1990.
>
> I enclose a signed copy of the contract of employment and look forward to seeing you on 1 March.
>
> Yours sincerely

Letters of Resignation

A *letter of resignation* should be written in good time for your employer to find a replacement for your job. The period of notice is usually stated in the contract of employment.

It is usual to give reasons why you are resigning though it is unnecessary to mention any increase in salary or wages. If you wish, you can write something friendly about the firm you are leaving but if your relationship with your head of department or colleagues has not been good, or if you feel hard done by in any way, do not write about it in your letter of resignation. Apart from the fact that it is not pleasant to leave a job on a discordant note, you may need a reference from your former employer at some time, so try to part on good terms.

Giving notice of resignation

> Dear Mr Smith
>
> According to the terms of my contract, I hereby give one month's notice to terminate my employment with Forth Pharmaceuticals Ltd on Friday, 30 November 1990.
>
> *(cont. overleaf)*

> The reason for my leaving is that I would like to widen my experience in the pharmaceutical business and am taking a position with a Swiss firm. I very much appreciate the opportunities I have had at Forth to gain research experience and shall remember my colleagues and work here with pleasure.
>
> Your sincerely

Useful phrases

Opening phrases

Please accept . . .

I hereby give . . . weeks/months notice according to the terms of my contract.

I would like to resign my position as . . .

Reasons for resigning

For some time now I have been anxious to move to a company where I could use my . . . training/skills.

My reason for leaving is that I would like to have more responsibility.

References and Testimonials

References are sometimes asked for along with an application for employment. These can be a general *testimonial* (also called an 'open letter of reference' or 'letter of recommendation') which an employee gets when leaving a firm, or a personal or 'character' reference which is written for a specific application. In the latter case, always ask someone before you give their name as a reference.

References and testimonials should be neither too enthusiastic nor indifferent but should simply and clearly state the facts about the person's character and/or work as far as they are known to you.

There are four essential points to keep in mind when writing a testimonial letter:

- refer to the person about whom you are writing in the first sentence or in an attention line;

- do not mention anything irrelevant to the position being applied for;
- do not be too enthusiastic;
- do not write anything libellous.

A testimonial begins with the salutation '*To whom it may concern*'. No complimentary close is needed. The name of the firm, signature of the writer and his or her position in the firm should be put at the bottom of the testimonial.

Reference for a member of staff

Dear Mr Jones

GRAHAM THINN

Thank you for your letter of 26 November asking for a reference for Graham Thinn.

Mr Thinn was employed by Quickline Office Equipment as a salesman from 1 March 1967 to 30 September 1974. He resigned in order to take up a position in Lancaster, his home town. During his period of employment with us his sales record was excellent. We were, in fact, sorry to lose him, as he was one of our best salesmen.

Throughout his employment with Quickline, his health, timekeeping and attendance record were all exemplary.

Yours sincerely

Reference for a personal friend

Dear Mr Brown

Thank you for your letter of 26 November asking for a reference for Graham Thinn.

Mr Thinn and I have been friends since we moved to this estate sixteen years ago, where he immediately got involved in community activities. He started our amateur dramatic society and has run our local Scout Troup for the last five years. He is also a committed member of the Parent-Teacher Association. It goes without saying that he is also a great family man.

I am sure that Mr Thinn will be an asset to your organization.

Yours sincerely

Testimonial

To whom it may concern

Mr and Mrs George Brown were employed by us as general handyman and housekeeper respectively in June 1975 and worked for us until December 1982.

In the seven years that they worked for us, both Mr and Mrs Brown proved reliable and trustworthy. They were able to take on responsibility where necessary and acted on their own initiative to keep our office building in good repair and good order.

They are giving up their positions in order to return to their home town of Cardiff. Our company offers a whole-hearted recommendation.

Markham and Wright (Solicitors)
David Wright (Solicitor)

6

Making Arrangements:
Invitations; Appointments

Formal Invitations

Though many arrangements are made by telephone these days, there are occasions when only a written message will do. These include formal invitations and, occasionally, asking for or confirming appointments.

Formal invitations can be sent either in the form of a letter or a card.

Formal invitation cards may be printed to specification or mass-produced with gaps to be filled in by the sender. They are always written in the third person:

Mr and Mrs Frank Smith request the pleasure of the company of *Ms Lucy Brown* . . .

Invitation cards are never dated. Likewise, there is no salutation or complimentary close. They often carry the abbreviation RSVP – répondez vous s'il vous plaît (French for *please reply*).

When having invitation cards printed, do not forget to include:

- the name(s) of the person or people doing the inviting;
- the name(s) of the person or people being invited;
- the reason for the invitation;
- the date and time of the function; if the function should end at a special time, include it;
- the place of the function.

When sending an invitation by *letter*, write from your home or business address as appropriate and date your letter. The letter should begin with a salutation and end with a complimentary close. You may write in either the third person (see above) or the first and second person(s):

We are giving a party on 1 June and should like to invite *you*
. . .

Follow the checklist for invitation cards.

Replying to a Formal Invitation

You may *reply to a formal invitation card* with either a card or letter.

If you have received an invitation in the form of a *letter* you should reply by letter unless a phone number is also given. When replying to a formal invitation by letter, write from your home or business address as appropriate and date your letter. Write in the same person as the original invitation, ie in either the third person:

Ms Lucy Brown thanks *Mr and Mrs Frank Smith* for their kind invitation and has much pleasure in accepting

or the first and second person(s), in which case you should begin the letter with a salutation and end with a complimentary close.

Note the use of the present tense – *has*. The invitation is being accepted now so the use of the future tense * *will have* would be wrong.

If you wish to *decline an invitation* give a reason for doing so. This should be both polite and plausible.

Invitation card

Mr Richard Wilson

requests the pleasure of the company of

Mr and Mrs David Wright

on the occasion of the opening of

The Wilson Gallery
15 Market Street
Yorkford YK6 5CX

on Wednesday, 2 May 1990
from 7.30 pm until 10.00 pm

RSVP

Accepting the invitation opposite

> Mr and Mrs David Wright thank Mr Richard Wilson for
> his kind invitation to the opening of the Wilson Gallery on
> 2 May and have much pleasure in accepting.

Declining the invitation opposite

> Mr and Mrs David Wright thank Mr Richard Wilson for
> his kind invitation to the opening of the Wilson Gallery
> to be held on 2 May 1990 but regret that they are unable
> to attend due to a prior engagement.

An invitation in the form of a letter

> Dear Dr Lawson
>
> Mr Roland Frame, the chairman of Bell Telecommuni-
> cations, and I are giving a cocktail party to welcome
> David Parsons, the head of our subsidiary in New York,
> who arrives for a short visit on 10 July. The party will be
> held on Saturday, 14 July at the Riding House Hotel,
> beginning at 7.00 pm.
>
> We hope that you will be able to join us and look forward
> to seeing you then.
>
> Yours sincerely

Accepting the invitation above

> Dear Ms Kellman
>
> Thank you very much for the invitation to cocktails at
> the Riding House Hotel on 14 July 1990. I am delighted
> to accept.
>
> Yours sincerely

Declining the invitation on page 77

> Dear Ms Kellman
>
> Thank you very much for the invitation to cocktails at the Riding House Hotel on 14 July 1990 to meet Mr David Parsons, head of your subsidiary in New York.
>
> I would be delighted to accept, but I have already made arrangements to attend another meeting on that date.
>
> Please pass on my regrets to Mr Parsons and give him my regards.
>
> Yours sincerely

Useful phrases

Mr and Mrs . . . have pleasure in inviting Mr and Ms . . .

Mr and Ms . . . request the pleasure of the company of Mr and Mrs . . .

We have pleasure in inviting you to attend a reception . . .

I would like to invite you to . . . on (date) at (time)/ . . . to dinner on Saturday, (date) at (time).

We hope you will be able to join us.

Accepting/declining an invitation

I have pleasure in accepting your invitation to dinner on . . . (date).

I was very pleased to get your invitation.

I regret that I have another arrangement at this time and will not be able to attend.

Unfortunately, business commitments will make it impossible for me to come to the meeting on . . . (date).

Appointments

When making an appointment by letter:

- always state the date and the day;
- do not forget the time of the appointment;
- offer an alternative time and date, if appropriate;
- ask for the appointment to be confirmed if necessary.

Asking for an appointment

Dear Mr Wright

I will be in London for a short visit from Monday, 27 August until Friday, 31 August and would like to meet you for a brief discussion at some time during the week.

I shall be staying at the Alhambra Hotel, Regent Street, and can easily come to your office at any time which is suitable for you. Please let me know when my visit would be convenient.

Yours sincerely

Making an appointment

Dear Mr Stevens

Thank you for your letter of 6 August 1990 asking for an appointment to see me. I am very much looking forward to renewing our acquaintanceship after such a long time and would like to suggest that you come to my office on Tuesday, 28 August at 11.30. If you have made no other arrangements, perhaps we could have lunch together after our discussion.

Yours sincerely

Useful phrases

I should like to suggest a meeting at . . . (time) on . . . (day and date) at my office.

Would it be convenient for you to meet me on . . . (day and date) at . . . (time)?

I hope to arrive in . . . on . . . (date) and shall call you from the airport.

My secretary will call you next week to arrange the date and time of our meeting.

Please confirm/let me know as soon as possible whether the date is convenient.

If you suggest a time, I shall try to fit the appointment into my schedule.

7

Thank-You Letters

Thanking someone for hospitality or for a present is often only a matter of a telephone call. There are, however, certain occasions when a letter is expected: for a wedding gift, or a present from colleagues, for example, or for hospitality from a business acquaintance. Try to write thank-you letters in a light, informal style as if you were speaking; you may use abbreviations like 'don't', 'can't', etc.

When *writing to thank someone for a present*:

- write the letter by hand;
- mention the present, saying what it was, etc; if you do not do this, the giver may think you have forgotten what he or she gave you;
- if you are writing to colleagues, write from your home address and address the envelope to the manager or head of staff; the inside address should include everyone, eg 'To the manager and staff';
- you may include anything else which is appropriate.

When *thanking someone for hospitality*:

- thank the person for their hospitality;
- compliment the host or hostess, if appropriate;
- offer to return the hospitality.

Thanks for a present

> To the manager and all the staff at 'The Diner'
>
> Mike and I would like to thank you all for the beautiful table-cloth and napkins which you gave us. Of all the
>
> *(cont. overleaf)*

farewell presents which we were given, this was one of the nicest.

You'll be pleased to hear that the removal went fine – nothing got broken and we didn't lose anything. Mike's new job is interesting but I'm still looking for work. I have an interview next week at the Job Centre. Whatever job they come up with, I bet it won't be as much fun as working at 'The Diner' for the last four years!

Mike sends his best wishes. We're both looking forward to seeing you all next summer.

Best wishes to all.

Thanks for hospitality

Dear Mr and Mrs James

Many thanks for your hospitality during my visit to Manchester. It was very kind of you to give me so much of your valuable time, especially when you have such a lot to do.

I hope that I may be able to return your kindness any time that you are in London.

Yours sincerely

Useful phrases
Thanks for gifts

Many thanks for the . . . which you sent me/which arrived last week.

I was so pleased to get the lovely . . .

We were delighted with the . . . which you gave us.

Appropriate extras

The wedding/removal went off without a hitch.

We had a lovely day for the wedding.

We were sorry that you couldn't come to the wedding.

Thanks for hospitality

It was very kind of you to invite me for dinner last week/ on . . . (day)/when I was visiting . . . (place).

I very much enjoyed meeting your husband and family.

I enjoyed myself/the meal/the show on . . . (day) tremendously/very much.

Returning hospitality

I/We hope to be able to return your hospitality/kindness soon.

I/We shall be very pleased to see you any time you are in . . . (place).

My wife is looking forward to meeting you when you come to . . . (place) next month.

8

Travelling: Arranging Accommodation

When *writing to a tourist information office* to ask about accommodation:

- be specific about the type of accommodation you want, stating whether you are interested in bed and breakfast accommodation, hotels or guest-houses;
- give the dates when you will need the accommodation.

When *writing an enquiry to a hotel or guest-house* it is important to:

- give details about the number of rooms and beds you want; if you are willing to accept alternative accommodation, mention it;
- state if you want an en suite shower/wc or bathroom;
- state how many nights you want the room for; give dates and days;
- ask about prices.

When *booking accommodation* do not forget to ask for confirmation of booking.

Writing to an information office to enquire about recommended hotels

> Dear Sir/Madam
>
> My husband and I would like to spend the first two weeks in August in York with our two children (thirteen and sixteen years old) and would be most grateful if you
>
> (*cont. on next page*)

would send us details of good hotels near the town centre.

Any information you can send us about the city itself and the surrounding countryside, including places of historical interest, will be very much appreciated.

Yours faithfully

Enquiring about prices

Dear Sir/Madam

I would like to enquire about the price of bed and breakfast in your guest-house from 15 to 30 August.

We are a family of four, two adults and two teenage daughters, and would like one double room and two single rooms, all with shower/wc. We would be willing to accept two double rooms, if that is all you have available at the above time.

I would be pleased to hear from you as soon as possible.

Yours faithfully

Booking accommodation

Dear Sir/Madam

Please reserve one single room with bath or shower from Friday, 9 November 1990 to Monday, 12 November 1990.

I expect to arrive early on Friday afternoon and will leave on Monday morning.

Kindly confirm this booking by return.

Yours faithfully

Useful phrases

Enquiring about accommodation

I will be in . . . (place) from . . . (day and date) to . . . (day and date).

I would like to have a list of first-class hotels in the . . . area.

Please send me information about reasonably priced hotels/ bed and breakfast accommodation/guest-houses in . . . (place).

Booking accommodation

Please reserve . . . room(s) for . . . night(s).

I would like to reserve a . . . room with bath/shower for . . . night(s) from . . . (day and date) to . . . (day and date).

I expect to arrive at the hotel at . . . (time) on . . . (day and date) and shall be leaving immediately after breakfast on . . . (day and date).

Please enclose a copy of your prices with your reply.

Please confirm this booking as soon as possible.

9

Letters of Condolence

A letter of condolence, whether to a colleague, friend or relation, is never easy to write. Even if we are not affected personally by the death, the taboos surrounding the subject in Western society make it difficult for us to put pen to paper. If you have to write a letter of condolence, remember that it will be more comforting to the recipient of the letter if you write in a simple, straightforward way using everyday words and phrases. Do not make the mistake of using euphemisms like 'passed away' or 'sleeping'. In the case of death after a long illness, phrases like 'blessed release' or 'happy release' may not be suitable.

A letter of condolence should be handwritten. It should be written as soon as you have heard of the death and should contain *only* your expression of sympathy and offer of help, if appropriate. Other messages or business should be left aside for a week or two.

Follow this basic pattern:

1. Address the recipient by name.
2. Begin the letter by saying that you are sorry to hear of the death and add in the case of sudden death, that it was a shock.
3. Continue with a second paragraph, which should be about the dead person and those he or she has left behind; you can say how much he or she will be missed.
4. End the letter by expressing condolence and, if the recipient is a close friend or relative, offering help.
5. Close the letter with 'Yours sincerely' if writing to a business acquaintance or 'With best wishes' or 'With kindest regards' etc if writing to a friend or relative.

You should mention God or prayers *only* if you are certain that the recipient of the letter is a believer and you, too, have the same beliefs.

Letter of condolence to a business acquaintance

> Dear Mr Davis
>
> We were deeply distressed to hear of the sudden death of your director, James Green.
>
> His death is a great loss to your firm and its associates. We who knew him will remember him not only as a knowledgeable businessman, but also as a humorous and kind person.
>
> My staff join me in sending our condolences to you and members of his family.
>
> Yours sincerely

Letter of condolence to the wife of a friend

> Dear Mrs Forbes,
>
> I was sorry to hear of George's death last week.
>
> I am sure you know how well liked and respected George was in our club. He will be greatly missed.
>
> Please accept my sympathy and heartfelt condolences and be sure to let me know if there is anything I can do to help you.
>
> With kindest regards

Useful phrases
Opening paragraph
I was/We were shocked to hear of the death of . . .
I/We have just learned of the death of . . .
I was/We were very sorry to hear the news about . . .

Second paragraph
. . . was always well respected/liked.
He/She will be greatly missed.
His/Her death is a great loss.

Last paragraph
Please accept my/our sympathy.
Please accept my/our sincere condolences.
If I/we can help in any way please do not hesitate to get in
    touch.
My thoughts are with you at this sad time.

Closing phrases
With best wishes
Sincere regards
With kindest regards
Yours very sincerely

10

Filling in Forms

Although the number of forms which we have to fill in throughout our lives is increasing, our ability to fill them it properly does not seem to get any better. Here are a few suggestions about how to deal with filling in forms.

1. Read the form through carefully from beginning to end before you start filling it in.
2. Reread the instructions telling you *how* to fill in the form and follow these instructions carefully, deleting or circling words or phrases, marking boxes with a cross or a tick or filling in an appropriate word or phrase as asked. If you do not follow the instructions, the chances are that the form will be sent back to you.
3. Always use black or blue ink and make definite deletions, crosses, etc. If written answers are asked for, *print* them clearly. You may use a typewriter, unless instructed otherwise. If a signature is needed, this must be handwritten.
4. If you are having difficulties ask for help from the place where you got the form.